SCIENTIFIC RIVALRIES
AND SCANDALS

BATTLE
OF THE
DINOSAUR
BONES

OTHNIEL CHARLES MARSH
VS EDWARD DRINKER COPE

REBECCA L. JOHNSON

Twenty-First Century Books
Minneapolis

For bone hunters and mystery lovers

Twenty-First Century Books
A division of Lerner Publishing Group, Inc.
241 First Avenue North
Minneapolis, MN 55401 U.S.A.

Website address: www.lernerbooks.com

Library of Congress Cataloging-in-Publication Data

Johnson, Rebecca L.
    Battle of the dinosaur bones : Othniel Charles Marsh vs.
Edward Drinker Cope / by Rebecca L. Johnson.
        p.   cm. — (Scientific rivalries and scandals)
    Includes bibliographical references and index.
    ISBN 978–0–7613–5488–8 (lib. bdg. : alk. paper)
    1. Paleontology—United States—History—19th
century—Juvenile literature. 2. Marsh, Othniel
Charles, 1831–1899—Juvenile literature. 3. Cope, E.
D. (Edward Drinker), 1840–1897—Juvenile literature.
4. Paleontologists—United States—Biography—Juvenile
literature. I. Title.
QE714.5.J635 2013
560.97309′034—dc23   2011045648

Manufactured in the United States of America
1 – MG – 7/15/12

CONTENTS

CHAPTER ONE

A BITTER RIVALRY

It was winter 1863. Two men were deep in conversation in a café near the heart of Berlin, Germany's capital city. Twenty–three–year–old Edward Drinker Cope hailed from Philadelphia, Pennsylvania.

He spoke passionately and gestured excitedly. The other man was Othniel Charles Marsh from New Haven, Connecticut. Nine years older than Cope, Marsh was quieter but equally intense. Cope and Marsh had only recently met, but they'd certainly heard about each other. They were rising stars in the new scientific field of paleontology, the study of ancient plant and animal fossils. Fossils—preserved remains or traces of ancient living things—reveal the history of life on Earth.

By the time they met in 1863, Edward Drinker Cope *(left)* and Othniel Charles Marsh *(right)* had each spent months visiting museums and universities across Europe, poring over fossil collections. Both were determined to become world-famous paleontologists.

A CHANGING WORLDVIEW

Until the 1700s, most Europeans and Americans believed that God had created Earth about six thousand years earlier. In their view, the familiar plants, animals, and other organisms that populated the planet had been present since Creation and remained unchanged ever since. Then scientists began studying geology, Earth's composition and shaping processes. New ideas about Earth's history emerged. In 1795 Scotsman James Hutton proposed that erosion and mountain building had been shaping Earth for much longer than six thousand years.

Geological studies also unearthed fossils that looked nothing like living organisms. In 1806 Frenchman Georges Cuvier proposed that some fossils were ancient organisms that had gone extinct. He noted that the older fossils were, the less they resembled modern organisms. Some of the strangest fossils unearthed in the early 1800s were those of enormous extinct reptiles. In 1841 Englishman Richard Owen coined the term *dinosaur* (terrible lizard) to describe them. These and other discoveries built a case for an ancient and changing Earth on which life itself gradually changes, or evolves.

In 1859 Englishman Charles Darwin published a key work called *On the Origin of Species by Means of Natural Selection*. In this book, Darwin proposed that organisms evolve through a process called natural selection. He explained how individuals better suited to their environment are more likely to survive, reproduce, and pass on their traits to their offspring. Through this process, populations of organisms change over time, and new types, or species, of organisms arise. Darwin presented a great deal of evidence to support his revolutionary theory.

ON

THE ORIGIN OF SPECIES

BY MEANS OF NATURAL SELECTION,

OR THE

PRESERVATION OF FAVOURED RACES IN THE STRUGGLE FOR LIFE.

By CHARLES DARWIN, M.A.,

FELLOW OF THE ROYAL, GEOLOGICAL, LINNÆAN, ETC., SOCIETIES;
AUTHOR OF 'JOURNAL OF RESEARCHES DURING H. M. S. BEAGLE'S VOYAGE
ROUND THE WORLD.'

LONDON:
JOHN MURRAY, ALBE
1859

The right

Charles Darwin's publication *On the Origin of Species by Means of Natural Selection* was first published in 1859. Darwin's ideas describing the process of evolution were among the great contributions to the field of biology.

Darwin acknowledged that the fossil record hadn't yet shown clear links between ancient organisms and more modern ones. He and others believed that intermediate forms would be found, though. Fossils were the key to supporting—or disproving—Darwin's theory. They were clues to Earth's past. For Cope and Marsh, fossils were also the path to fame.

FROM FRIEND TO FOE

In Berlin Cope and Marsh parted on friendly terms. However, jealousy, greed, and fierce competition soon drove them apart. Each strove to discover more fossils, name more species, and publish more papers than the other. Their bitter rivalry, known as the Bone Wars, dominated U.S. science for two decades. It even made newspaper headlines. Nasty as it was, the Bone Wars produced a treasure trove of fossils that laid a firm foundation for American paleontology. What's more, some of the discoveries were the evolutionary missing links Darwin and others predicted would be found. These fossils were proof that living things do evolve and that modern species descended from organisms that lived millions of years ago.

MARSH'S BEGINNINGS

Cope and Marsh came from very different backgrounds. Born October 29, 1831, Marsh grew up on a small farm near Lockport, New York. His mother died when he was three. Marsh and his older sister, Mary, became nearly inseparable. Quiet and standoffish, young Marsh had few friends. But he found a steadfast companion in his neighbor Ezekiel Jewett, a retired military colonel. Marsh and Jewett often hunted together. Jewett was an amateur geologist, so their outings included collecting interesting rocks and fossils.

By the time he was twenty, Marsh hadn't completed a high school education. A year later, he received an inheritance from his mother's estate, which was managed by her wealthy brother, George Peabody. Marsh decided to use the money to enroll at Phillips Andover Academy in Andover, Massachusetts. But Marsh's heart wasn't in his studies. He often skipped class to collect rocks and fossils—or play backgammon! That summer, though, Marsh's beloved sister Mary died in childbirth. Devastated, Marsh took stock of his life. Walking in the countryside near his sister's home, he decided to stop wasting his time. "I changed my mind during an afternoon spent on Dracut Heights," he said years later. "I resolved I would return to Andover, and take hold, and really study."

"I changed my mind [about my life] during an afternoon spent on Dracut Heights. I resolved I would return to Andover, take hold, and really study."

O. C. Marsh, 1852

Marsh worked hard at school for the first time in his life. He discovered he liked competing with others and that he had a knack for outsmarting opponents. Science—geology in particular—became his passion. And he made time for collecting. During a rock-hunting trip in Canada in 1855, he found what looked like two fossil fish vertebrae (backbone segments) on the cliffs of the Bay of Fundy. He pocketed them for later study.

After graduating from Andover, Marsh decided to continue his education at Yale College in New Haven. Uncle George Peabody, impressed by his nephew's achievements, paid his way. Marsh excelled at Yale, and when he graduated in 1860, he received a scholarship for graduate study. His choice was Yale's prestigious Sheffield Scientific School, where he signed up for advanced classes in chemistry, physics, geology, and botany.

During his graduate studies, Marsh showed the fossil vertebrae he'd collected in Canada to his geology professor. The professor suggested Marsh send them to Harvard University professor Louis Agassiz, a world expert on fossil fishes. Agassiz concluded the bones were from an unknown, extinct animal that had both fish and amphibian traits.

The Bay of Fundy, where Marsh collected fossils in 1855, is in northeastern Canada. It has the highest tides in the world.

Not wanting Agassiz to take credit for his discovery, Marsh demanded the fossils back. He carried out his own analysis and decided that Agassiz was wrong. The bones, he believed, were from a creature related to ichthyosaurs, ancient sea reptiles. Marsh named it *Eosaurus acadianus*.

WHAT'S
IN A NAME?

Scientists classify organisms (group them into categories) based on their similarities. The smallest category is the species. Members of the same species can mate and produce fertile offspring. A genus consists of similar species. Together, the genus and species names make up an organism's scientific name. Using mostly Latin and Greek words, a scientific name describes the organism, its discovery, or both. Take *Eosaurus acadianus* as an example. *Eosaurus* means "early lizard," while *acadianus* refers to Acadia, the region where Marsh found the fossil. Whoever discovers a species usually gets the honor of naming it.

After completing his graduate degree, Marsh persuaded his uncle George to donate a large sum of money to Yale to establish a world-class science museum. The university showed its appreciation by creating the first U.S. professorship of paleontology and offering Marsh the job. In fall 1862, Marsh headed to Europe to prepare for his new position. He visited Charles Darwin and other prominent European scientists, studied paleontology at several German universities, and purchased fossils for the new Peabody Museum of Natural History. And—he met Edward Cope.

CHILD PRODIGY

Born into a wealthy Quaker family on July 28, 1840, Cope grew up near Philadelphia, Pennsylvania. He was an energetic child with a keen interest in nature—and a near-photographic memory. By the age of six, Cope was drawing accurate pictures of plants and animals. By eight, he was attending a Quaker school and mastering every subject. Cope made friends easily, but he had a fiery temper.

Philadelphia was home to the Academy of Natural Sciences, a prestigious center of U.S. natural science research. When Cope wasn't in school, he haunted the academy's museum, learning about the items on display. At home, he started his own collections of rocks and fossils.

In 1853 Cope began attending an elite Quaker boarding school in Westtown, Pennsylvania. He excelled in everything but was bored. That frustration was coupled with his father's insistence that Cope abandon his studies and manage the family's estate. When Cope turned sixteen, his father demanded he train for a life as a gentleman farmer by working at farms around Philadelphia. Cope complied but continued his nature studies in his spare time. In 1859 he published his first scientific paper—on two new species of salamanders he'd discovered—in the academy's journal.

In 1860 Cope's father gave in, and Cope attended lectures in comparative anatomy at the University of Pennsylvania. Comparative anatomy is the study of similarities and differences in the structure of organisms. The lecturer was Joseph Leidy, the foremost U.S. anatomist and vertebrate paleontologist.

The Academy of Natural Sciences in Philadelphia, Pennsylvania, is the oldest natural history museum in the United States. It was founded in 1812.

Fossil vertebrates, as well as modern reptiles, amphibians, and fish, quickly became Cope's specialty. While in Washington, D.C., where he was studying the Smithsonian Institution's collection of reptiles and amphibians, he wrote to his sister, "I have very interesting times talking to the various learned persons who haunt this place. I can learn something every second."

When Cope wasn't studying, he wrote. By the age of twenty-one, he had published thirty-one scientific papers. By the time he met Marsh in Berlin in 1863, Cope's unconventional education had made him an expert in vertebrates, both living and extinct.

> "I have very interesting times talking to the various learned persons who haunt this place. I can learn something every second."
>
> E. D. Cope, describing the Smithsonian Institution, January 4, 1863

CHAPTER TWO

COMPETITION

By 1866 Marsh and Cope were back in the United States. Marsh had settled in at Yale, where Peabody money funded his professorship.

Still single, he devoted all his time to paleontology. Cope, on the other hand, had married a distant cousin, Annie Pim, and had a baby daughter, Julia. He worked as a zoology professor at Haverford College near Philadelphia.

Cope enjoyed teaching, but he preferred to collect fossils. His favorite spot for collecting was Haddonfield, New Jersey. The area was famous for its deposits of claylike marl. Marl is ancient seafloor mud that was laid down during the Cretaceous period (145.5 to 65.5 million years ago), when ocean waters covered much of New Jersey.

Around Haddonfield, people dug up marl for fertilizer, often exposing Cretaceous fossils in the process. Most were small, but in the mid-1800s, large bones had been discovered. Several marl-digging companies had agreed to notify Cope of interesting fossil finds. In August 1866, J. C. Voorhees of the West Jersey Marl Company invited Cope to examine some recently unearthed bones.

Earth's Geologic Time Scale, Mesozoic to Present

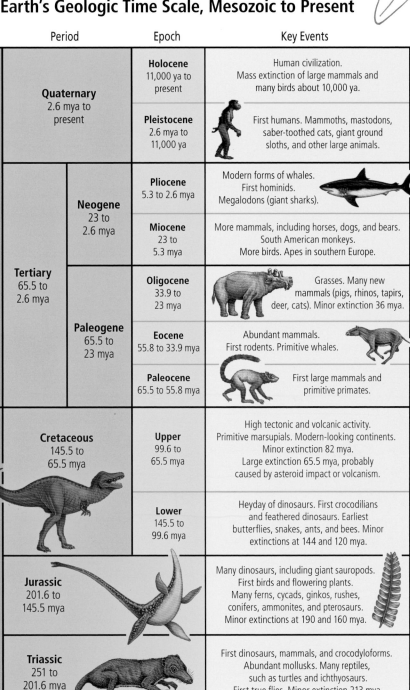

Era	Period		Epoch	Key Events
Cenozoic—65.5 mya to present	**Quaternary** 2.6 mya to present		**Holocene** 11,000 ya to present	Human civilization. Mass extinction of large mammals and many birds about 10,000 ya.
			Pleistocene 2.6 mya to 11,000 ya	First humans. Mammoths, mastodons, saber-toothed cats, giant ground sloths, and other large animals.
	Tertiary 65.5 to 2.6 mya	**Neogene** 23 to 2.6 mya	**Pliocene** 5.3 to 2.6 mya	Modern forms of whales. First hominids. Megalodons (giant sharks).
			Miocene 23 to 5.3 mya	More mammals, including horses, dogs, and bears. South American monkeys. More birds. Apes in southern Europe.
		Paleogene 65.5 to 23 mya	**Oligocene** 33.9 to 23 mya	Grasses. Many new mammals (pigs, rhinos, tapirs, deer, cats). Minor extinction 36 mya.
			Eocene 55.8 to 33.9 mya	Abundant mammals. First rodents. Primitive whales.
			Paleocene 65.5 to 55.8 mya	First large mammals and primitive primates.
Mesozoic—251 to 65.5 mya	**Cretaceous** 145.5 to 65.5 mya		**Upper** 99.6 to 65.5 mya	High tectonic and volcanic activity. Primitive marsupials. Modern-looking continents. Minor extinction 82 mya. Large extinction 65.5 mya, probably caused by asteroid impact or volcanism.
			Lower 145.5 to 99.6 mya	Heyday of dinosaurs. First crocodilians and feathered dinosaurs. Earliest butterflies, snakes, ants, and bees. Minor extinctions at 144 and 120 mya.
	Jurassic 201.6 to 145.5 mya			Many dinosaurs, including giant sauropods. First birds and flowering plants. Many ferns, cycads, ginkos, rushes, conifers, ammonites, and pterosaurs. Minor extinctions at 190 and 160 mya.
	Triassic 251 to 201.6 mya			First dinosaurs, mammals, and crocodyloforms. Abundant mollusks. Many reptiles, such as turtles and ichthyosaurs. First true flies. Minor extinction 213 mya.

Key: mya = million years ago; ya = years ago

THE HADDONFIELD
HADROSAUR

In 1858 amateur fossil hunter William Parker Foulke made a landmark find in a Haddonfield marl pit: a nearly complete dinosaur skeleton. He called in Joseph Leidy, who concluded that the dinosaur had walked upright on its massive hind legs. Leidy named the creature _Hadrosaurus foulkii_. It became the world's first mounted dinosaur skeleton, inspiring great public and academic interest in dinosaurs.

They turned out to be the partial remains of an 18-foot (5.5-meter) meat-eating dinosaur that was new to science. Cope named it _Laelaps aquilunguis_. Laelaps is a hunting dog in Greek mythology, and _aquilunguis_ means "having claws like an eagle's." Cope quickly penned a scientific paper about _Laelaps_—one Marsh was sure to have read.

Soon after, Cope resigned from Haverford College and devoted himself full-time to paleontology. In spring 1868, he moved to Haddonfield to be closer to the marl beds. Around the same time, Marsh invited himself for a visit. The two paleontologists explored the marl pits together and discovered several small fossils. Marsh also met Voorhees. Without Cope's knowledge, Marsh struck a deal with the marl digger. The West Jersey Marl Company would now ship all interesting bones to Marsh.

COPE'S MISTAKE

A few months later, Marsh rode the new transcontinental railroad across the windswept Great Plains toward Wyoming. Along the route lay tiny Antelope Junction, Nebraska, where locals claimed to have found strange bones they believed were ancient "human remains." As the train approached the tiny station, Marsh persuaded the conductor to stop briefly so he could explore the bone site. There were indeed bones in the dusty sediments, but they weren't human. Marsh recognized them as fossils of several extinct reptiles and mammals. He hired the stationmaster to collect some of the bones for him and picked them up on the return trip. In the small collection were fossils of at least eleven different species of extinct animals. The ones that excited Marsh the most were those of a small, three-toed horse. He suspected it was an ancestor of modern horses, perhaps one of Darwin's missing links. He named it *Equus parvulus*.

Marsh returned to Yale to find a crate from Voorhees. It contained bones of a mosasaur, an immense ancient marine reptile. It wasn't long before Cope learned about the mosasaur—and Marsh's arrangement with Voorhees. He felt betrayed.

Yet Cope had something else on his mind. An army surgeon at Fort Wallace, Kansas, had sent several crates containing hundreds of fossil bones to the academy in Philadelphia. Cope determined the bones were those of a plesiosaur, an ancient marine reptile even bigger than Marsh's mosasaur. Plesiosaurs and mosasaurs had lived in a shallow ocean that covered central North America during the Cretaceous. The Kansas find was the largest and most complete plesiosaur fossil Cope had ever seen.

It took Cope almost a year to clean, sort, and assemble all the bones. The finished skeleton was nearly 35 feet (11 m) long. Cope named his plesiosaur *Elasmosaurus platyurus*. He published an article about it, complete with detailed illustrations, and sent copies to other paleontologists, including Marsh. In 1869, when Cope heard Marsh was coming to Philadelphia to see *Hadrosaurus foulkii*, he invited Marsh to see *Elasmosaurus platyurus* too. Here was Cope's chance to upstage the man who had "stolen" mosasaur fossils out of Cope's very backyard.

When Marsh arrived at the academy, Cope proudly showed off the *Elasmosaurus* skeleton. Marsh inspected it and then announced that Cope had made a serious error: he'd put the skull on the tail instead of the neck.

Insulted and indignant, Cope flatly disagreed. The argument grew heated, and the two men called in Leidy to settle their dispute.

Leidy examined the skeleton. Then he removed the skull, carried it to the other end of the skeleton, and slipped it into position. It fit perfectly. Marsh had been right. Cope was mortified.

To salvage his reputation, Cope tried to get back every copy of his *Elasmosaurus* paper. Marsh and Leidy refused to return theirs. At a March 1870 academy meeting, Leidy noted Cope's mistake. Leidy was diplomatic in also describing the importance of Cope's find. But the damage was done.

These events marked a turning point in Cope and Marsh's relationship. Simple competition had escalated to bitter animosity. The Bone Wars had begun.

FIRST YALE EXPEDITION

Marsh wanted to collect as many fossils as possible for the Peabody Museum. It would be best if he could return to the fossil-rich West before Cope. In spring 1870, Marsh began planning a fossil-hunting expedition to parts of Nebraska, Kansas, Colorado, Wyoming, and Utah. He called upon military friends for help. The railroad would take his team to army outposts. At each fort, the team would pick up a military escort for protection from Indian soldiers. The team would travel out from these forts on horseback—for weeks at a time—to search for fossils. George Peabody had recently died, leaving Marsh with plenty of money to finance the trip.

On June 30, 1870, Marsh and eleven Yale student volunteers left New Haven for Fort McPherson in western Nebraska. There they picked up horses, wagons, supplies, and the military escort. For the next two weeks, Marsh and his men traversed dry, rolling plains under a scorching sun in search of fossil treasures. On many days, the temperature soared over 100°F (38°C).

The rock in western Nebraska formed during the Pliocene epoch, about 5.3 million to 2.6 million years ago. By then, the inland sea that covered North America's interior during the Cretaceous had long since receded. Whenever Marsh spotted something interesting among the rocky hillsides, he stopped to investigate. If it looked promising, the students unloaded their tools and

Marsh poses (center) with the members of the 1870 Yale expedition. At this time, the United States had few roads. Train tracks had only recently been laid coast to coast. Marsh's team traveled by train to military forts and hunted fossils on horseback.

began to dig. They unearthed fossils of ancient camels, rhinoceroses, and at least six horse species that had once roamed the Pliocene plains.

Back at Fort McPherson, Marsh's men crated the fossils and sent them east to New Haven by train. Then they boarded a westbound train for Cheyenne, Wyoming, and picked up an escort at nearby Fort Russell.

Throughout August, Marsh and his Yalies circled through the West. In Colorado they discovered fossils of turtles, rhinoceroses, oreodonts (sheeplike plant eaters), birds, and brontotheres (rhinolike plant-eaters) that had lived during the Eocene epoch, about 55.8 million to 33.9 million years ago. During the Eocene, mammals were beginning to diversify and spread across North America. In western Nebraska, the men swung through Antelope Junction, and Marsh was delighted to find bones of three more prehistoric horse species.

Fort Bridger in western Wyoming was the base for the expedition's next leg. En route to Utah, Marsh and his men passed through Bridger Basin, Wyoming. Hunters and local Indians claimed that this desolate region of dry buttes and windswept plains was littered with enormous bones. But Marsh found only small fossils.

A STRANGE BONE

For the last leg of the expedition, Marsh returned to western Kansas. Bitter November winds buffeted the men as they scoured the chalky Cretaceous rocks along the Smoky Hill River. Cope's *Elasmosaurus* had come from this area. Marsh was determined to find a plesiosaur of his own—bigger and better than Cope's. Although he did discover bones of a mosasaur nearly 15 feet (4.6 m) long, Marsh found no plesiosaurs. He was bitterly disappointed.

On the last day of exploration, however, Marsh found a small bone along the riverbank. It was as long as his palm and hollow, like the bone of a bird. But it had a very unbirdlike joint at one end. In camp, Marsh puzzled over the fossil. He knew it was important—and that he'd have to wait until he was back at Yale to analyze it carefully.

Thirty-six huge crates of fossils awaited Marsh at Yale. He spent months studying them and by early 1871 had published papers on the key finds. The birdlike bone turned out to be one of the most exciting discoveries. It was from the wing of a pterodactyl, a flying reptile from the Cretaceous or earlier. Marsh's pterodactyl was the largest found to date. "I therefore made a careful calculation of how large a Pterodactyl must be to have a wing finger corresponding to the fragment I had found," he wrote, "and ascertained [determined] that its spread of wings would be about 20 feet [6 m]—truly a gigantic dragon even in this country of big things."

Scientists all over the country read Marsh's scientific papers about the amazing discoveries. Newspapers ran stories too, sparking fossil fever—and

Pterodactyls were flying reptiles with long, narrow heads and almost one hundred large teeth. They had long necks and large, leathery wings.

"I therefore made a careful calculation of how large a Pterodactyl must be to have a wing finger corresponding to the fragment I had found, and ascertained [determined] that its spread of wings would be about 20 feet [6 m]—truly a gigantic dragon even in this country of big things."

O. C. Marsh, 1871

spotlighting the accomplishments of O. C. Marsh.

Meanwhile, in Philadelphia, Cope was trying to figure out how to compete. He lacked the money to mount a large fossil-hunting expedition, and he had no military connections. But Cope knew if he didn't get to the West soon, he'd never catch up with Marsh.

Cope saw an opportunity in the U.S. government's new geological surveys. These were large, multiyear expeditions through the western United States. Survey mapmakers, geologists, and other scientists created detailed maps, assessed natural resources, and conducted other research. The surveys offered many fossil-hunting opportunities. And the government paid to publish each survey's scientific findings.

Four surveys were under way in the early 1870s. Cope wanted to join geologist Ferdinand Hayden's survey of the High Plains. He knew that Hayden had sent Leidy many interesting fossils. Cope hoped his friendship with Leidy would help him land a job with the Hayden survey. But by summer 1871, he had not yet received a job offer. Cope sat stranded in Philadelphia.

SECOND YALE EXPEDITION

Marsh returned to Fort Wallace, Kansas, with another team of Yale students in early July 1871. He wanted to find more of the huge pterodactyl's skeleton. The team found the spot along the Smoky Hill River where Marsh had made the discovery the year before. There they found more of the giant winged creature's bones plus skeletons of several more pterodactyls.

THE GREAT
WESTERN SURVEYS

After the Civil War (1861–1865), four major surveys covered large parts of the western United States. From 1867 to 1873, Clarence King's team explored along the route of the transcontinental railroad, from eastern Wyoming to western Nevada. The Hayden survey (1871–1877) traveled through vast areas of Nebraska, Colorado, and Wyoming, including what would become Yellowstone National Park. John Wesley Powell's team trekked through canyons and along rivers in the southwestern United States from 1870 to 1876. Powell named the Grand Canyon, and he and his men were the first whites to raft down the Colorado River. Finally, George Wheeler's survey (1869–1879) attempted to map all U.S. territory from 100° west longitude to the Pacific Ocean.

In late August, the expedition headed to Wyoming. They spent six weeks exploring the Bridger Basin. This time Marsh found massive fossils. They lay exposed on the ground or jutted out of hillsides of chalky Eocene rock. Most belonged to prehistoric mammals, such as early forms of rhinos, elephants, and tapirs. Marsh was especially pleased when he discovered two more species of ancient horse. As far as Marsh was concerned, every bone in the basin was his.

COPE GOES ALONE

When news of Marsh's second expedition reached Cope, he decided to go to western Kansas by himself, at his own expense. Arriving at Fort Wallace in early September, he hired a wagon, mules, supplies, and a five-man military guard.

Cope started along the banks of the Smoky Hill River. Gradually he figured out the best places to look. He scoured ravines and creek beds where running water had carried fossils into low spots. He scrambled along riverbanks and cliffs where wind and rain had exposed bones embedded in the rock.

Cope roamed western Kansas for several weeks. He unearthed fossils of plesiosaurs, mosasaurs, huge fish, and sea turtles—and pterodactyls. One specimen had a wingspan of 25 feet (7.6 m). Cope was thrilled. He'd found a pterodactyl bigger than Marsh's! He wrote to his wife, "The stories I hear of what Marsh and others have found is something wonderful, and I can now tell my own stories, which for the time I have been here are not bad."

"I can now tell my own stories, which for the time I have been here are not bad."

E. D. Cope, after discovering more pterodactyl fossils, September 21, 1871

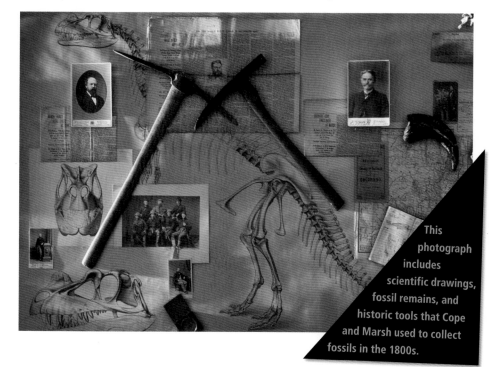

This photograph includes scientific drawings, fossil remains, and historic tools that Cope and Marsh used to collect fossils in the 1800s.

CHAPTER THREE

BRIDGER
BASIN

In spring 1872, Cope was finally appointed chief paleontologist of the Hayden survey. Hayden intended to explore western Wyoming—and Bridger Basin—that summer.

It was precisely where Cope wanted to go. As Marsh had discovered, fossils in the basin offered a remarkable view of life on North America's Eocene plains. The extinct animals that had roamed those plains shared key traits with modern species. Such similarities supported Darwin's ideas of gradual evolutionary change. And because Bridger Basin was absolutely littered with fossils, chances of discovering new species of extinct animals—and becoming famous in the process—were great.

Cope's high spirits were dashed when he arrived at Fort Bridger in mid-June. Hayden's team had left without him. He was stuck at the fort until he could get enough money to buy or rent what he needed. Frantic, he wrote to his father and to Hayden for funds.

News of Cope's arrival in Wyoming soon reached Marsh. Marsh knew Cope would eventually get out into the field, particularly Bridger Basin. But Marsh didn't want to leave Yale just then. He was writing up his research on the fossils he'd collected the previous year—and struggling to keep pace with Cope's prolific publications. So he took steps to hinder his rival's fossil hunting. Marsh hired two men, John Chew and Sam Smith, to collect fossils in Wyoming over the next few months and also keep an eye on Cope. He told them to keep Cope out of the best fossil areas.

For weeks, Cope waited at Fort Bridger. Annie and Julia arrived to keep him company. When Cope finally could buy horses and supplies in mid-July, he hurriedly hired a cook and two assistants and headed out into Bridger Basin. It was hard going, but within just a few days he had found fossils from thirty different types of extinct animals. Many were new species. Cope wrote to Annie about his finds. He told her to keep the news quiet because he didn't want Marsh to hear about his success.

Annie wrote back with news of her own: Joseph Leidy had arrived at Fort Bridger. Not wanting

Geologist Ferdinand Hayden *(eighth from left, seated at table)* was in charge of one of the great western surveys funded by the U.S. government after the Civil War. In this photo, he is pictured in Wyoming in the 1870s.

to cross paths with Leidy or share information about what he'd found, Cope moved his camp several miles away. There he came across a set of massive fossil bones that he initially thought were those of some enormous ancient mammal. But upon closer inspection, Cope realized he'd found a dinosaur, which he named *Agathaumas sylvestris* (marvelous forest dweller). He found enough bones to estimate that *Agathaumas* had weighed around 6 tons (5.4 metric tons). It was the largest dinosaur found in North America to date.

Cope worked feverishly to get as much done as possible. He rose before dawn and hunted for fossils until it was too dark to see. Each night he stayed up late, studying the day's finds and writing about them. Periodically, Cope returned to Fort Bridger to see his family, get supplies, and mail scientific papers to journals back east.

Cope's assistants were worthless, and he eventually fired them. Then he met Sam Smith, who claimed he was unhappy working for Marsh. Cope was happy to hire Smith away from Marsh—or so he thought.

ON BEING FIRST

In the 1870s, the fastest way to publish news of a discovery was to send brief letters or telegrams to scientific journals. Journals often published these announcements as separates, or short articles printed separately from the journal and mailed to interested scientists. Scientific societies also read separates into their meeting notes, which made the information part of the official scientific record. The date on which a separate or scientific paper was received, printed, or read aloud was critical. Whoever went on record first with a discovery got the credit—and the right to name a new species.

MARSH ARRIVES

Back at Yale, Marsh was getting uneasy about the developments at Bridger Basin. First, Cope had arrived, then Leidy. Then Smith, it seemed, had gone to work for his rival! In a letter to Marsh, Smith claimed he'd joined Cope to spy on him and to keep him away from Marsh's best fossil sites. Marsh didn't trust Smith, though. With four Yale students, he headed west.

Marsh made a brief stop in western Kansas to explore the Smoky Hill River region again. His team found fossils of several large flightless birds, including one more than 5 feet (1.5 m) tall. Marsh named it *Hesperornis regalis*, or "royal western bird." *Hesperornis* turned out to be a key fossil find because its beak was lined with small lizardlike teeth. An extinct bird with reptilian traits was important evidence in support of Darwin's theory of evolution.

Marsh's team found fossil remains of *Hesperornis regalis* in rocks of the Cretaceous period in western Kansas. The extinct waterbird had teeth and long legs for swimming. This is Marsh's 1880 reconstruction of the fossil.

EVIDENCE
FOR EVOLUTION

Darwin had predicted that if life evolved as he proposed, then the fossil record should contain intermediate life-forms that linked major groups of living things. *Hesperornis* was just such an intermediate form, with characteristics common to both birds and reptiles. *Hesperornis* was strong evidence that birds and reptiles had evolved from a common ancestor at some point in Earth's history. Marsh's discovery of *Hesperornis* fit together well with the 1861 discovery in Europe of another intermediate form called *Archaeopteryx* (ancient wing), a small dinosaur with feather-covered wings.

Then Marsh made a beeline for Wyoming. For most of August, Cope and Marsh worked a few miles apart in Bridger Basin. Yet they never crossed paths, and Leidy avoided them both. The top three U.S. paleontologists were all digging in the same area, in deposits of roughly the same age—and not communicating at all.

TRIPLE TROUBLE

James Carter, an amateur naturalist living at Fort Bridger, occasionally joined Leidy on his fossil-hunting trips. One day Carter and another man found some huge fossil bones. Leidy determined that they belonged to a very large, rhinoceros-like mammal. He called it *Uintatherium robustum* (strong beast of the Uintas), referring to the nearby Uinta Mountains. Leidy described the fossil find in a letter to the Academy of Natural Sciences in Philadelphia. A member of the academy read Leidy's letter during a meeting at the end of July. The letter was set to be published as a short article on August 1, 1872.

In mid-August, Cope came across fossils that also appeared to be from a huge, rhinolike mammal. Its massive skull had tusks and three sets of horns. Cope named it *Loxolophodon cornutus* (slanting crested horn). On August 17, he sent a telegram to the American Philosophical Society announcing *Loxolophodon*'s discovery.

A few miles from Cope's site, Marsh unearthed four sets of fossils of huge animals with three sets of horns and tusklike teeth. Marsh believed they were four closely related species and named them *Dinoceras mirabile*, *Dinoceras lacustris*, *Tinoceras anceps*, and *Tinoceras grandis*. He sent his first bulletin about these new fossils to a scientific journal on August 19.

Both Leidy and Marsh went back east in September. Cope kept working at breakneck speed, though, until his exhausting search for more and better fossils took its toll. He returned to Fort Bridger in mid-September with a raging fever and a deep cough. Annie nursed her husband until he was well enough to travel home at the end of October.

By late fall, the three paleontologists' articles on their Bridger Basin discoveries began appearing in scientific journals. It became obvious that Leidy's *Uintatherium*, Marsh's *Dinoceras* and *Tinoceras*, and Cope's *Loxolophodon* were the same or very similar animals (later called

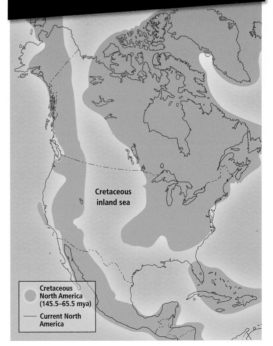

This map shows the modern outlines of North America over the land as it was during the Cretaceous period. Marsh and Cope found many fossils from this geologic time period.

Cretaceous inland sea

Cretaceous North America (145.5–65.5 mya)

Current North America

uintatheres). Almost immediately, Marsh and Cope began bickering over who had found which fossils when and, therefore, who had a right to name these new species and get credit for their discovery. By January 1873, an all-out war of words was under way. Cope and Marsh sent each other nasty letters. Each accused the other of inventing information and falsifying dates. The fight became public when it moved into scientific journals, including the respected *American Naturalist*.

In the March 1873 issue, for example, Cope said uintatheres probably were ancestors of modern elephants. Marsh wrote a sneering rebuttal: "Prof. Cope . . . has made several serious mistakes in his observations. He has likewise been especially unfortunate in attributing to the Dinocerata [uintatheres] characters which they do not possess; and hence his conclusion, that all these animals . . . possessed a proboscis [nose], is quite erroneous. In his references and dates, also, Professor Cope also has shown the same inaccuracy that has marred his scientific work."

In a May 1873 article, Cope restated his ancestor-of-elephants claim. He said he wasn't responsible for date errors made by printers and secretaries while he was in the field. He claimed he'd found *Loxolophodon* at least a month before

> "Prof. Cope... has made several serious mistakes in his observations. He has likewise been especially unfortunate in attributing to the Dinocerata [uintatheres] characters which they do not possess; and hence his conclusion, that all these animals... possessed a proboscis [nose], is quite erroneous. In his references and dates, also, Professor Cope has shown the same inaccuracy that has marred his scientific work."
>
> O. C. Marsh, in *American Naturalist*, March 1873

Marsh had unearthed *Dinoceras*. He wrote, "It is plain that most of Prof. Marsh's criticisms are misrepresentations ... and his statements as to the dates of my papers are either criminally ambiguous or untrue."

The battle became an unprofessional spectacle. Never before had U.S. scholars behaved so childishly. Leidy was appalled and began to distance himself from Cope and Marsh.

The *American Naturalist* had also had enough. In the June 1873 issue, the editors invited both paleontologists to publish a final essay at their own expense. Cope wrote one condescending, dismissive paragraph. Marsh's rebuttal was nine pages long and full of venom.

LEIDY AND THE UINTATHERES

Leidy quietly studied and compared all the uintathere fossils while Cope and Marsh squabbled. Leidy concluded that his *Uintatherium* was the same as Marsh's *Dinoceras*. He believed Cope's fossils were closely related species. Later studies showed Leidy was largely correct. After publishing his conclusions, Leidy withdrew almost completely from paleontology. He wanted nothing more to do with Cope and Marsh's juvenile, unprofessional behavior.

CHAPTER FOUR

DISTANT
ENEMIES

Cope and Marsh both headed west in summer 1873. Marsh mounted another Yale expedition, with eleven students and two scouts.

His first stop was Nebraska's Niobrara River. Its sandy bluffs yielded many interesting mammal fossils, including more species of prehistoric horses. Then Marsh returned to Bridger Basin. By summer's end, he had collected forty-nine large crates of fossils.

Cope had rejoined the Hayden survey. Accompanied by a small team of assistants, he started his fossil prospecting in northern Colorado and slowly moved into Wyoming, carefully avoiding Marsh. Late in the summer, he headed for the Platte River area in western Nebraska, exploring many of the same sites Marsh had already worked. Cope described his fossil finds in the survey's official report. He made cutting remarks about Marsh's discoveries in the text.

Irritated by Cope's criticisms, Marsh pressured Hayden to stop publishing Cope's papers. Hayden refused because Cope was an excellent paleontologist. In refusing, Hayden became Marsh's enemy too.

This ancient horse fossil (*Mesohippus*) is about 30 to 40 million years old. This type of horse was common in ancient North America. The fossil was found in Nebraska, where Marsh, too, found fossils of prehistoric horses.

In spring 1874, Marsh was elected to the prestigious National Academy of Sciences. (Cope was the only academy member to cast a "no" vote.) Marsh began networking with scientists, politicians, and other influential people. As the summer fossil-hunting season approached, Marsh decided to stay at Yale to analyze fossils and publish papers. He also wanted to oversee construction of the Peabody Museum of Natural History.

With the museum in mind, Marsh took a much more businesslike approach to bone hunting. He wanted more of certain types of fossils, such as birds with teeth and prehistoric horses. And he wanted as many fossils as possible. Marsh hired teams of fossil hunters to do most of his fieldwork. Two key collectors were Benjamin Mudge, a natural history professor and geologist from Kansas, and Sam Williston, one of Mudge's former students.

Marsh demanded absolute loyalty. (He had fired Sam Smith for switching sides.) He also expected secrecy. In this competitive environment, he didn't want news of his discoveries leaked to anyone—especially Cope.

MARSH'S FINAL EXPEDITION

In October 1874, an army general sent word of vast fossil deposits near the White River in northern Nebraska and southern Dakota Territory. Intrigued,

Marsh hastily put together a team of men and traveled by rail to Fort McPherson, Nebraska. They picked up horses and wagons and headed to the Red Cloud Agency.

The agency was a government office near the American Indian reservation where Chief Red Cloud and his large band of Oglala Sioux lived. Red Cloud had recently defeated the U.S. Army during a major battle in Wyoming. A treaty was signed. Red Cloud agreed to settle near the agency, which was charged with providing the tribe with food and essential supplies as well as helping keep the peace. But the government agents were corrupt and treated the Indians badly. Tensions were running high between Indians and whites.

When Marsh arrived, the Sioux angrily demanded that he and his men leave. The Indians believed Marsh had come looking for gold, as other white men had. Marsh refused to go. Instead, he met with Red Cloud and the other Sioux chiefs and explained that he was after ancient bones, not gold. Eventually persuaded, the tribal leaders gave Marsh permission to pass through their land to reach the White River Badlands (part of which forms modern Badlands National Park in South Dakota). There, centuries of erosion had carved the limestone sediments into steep bluffs and deep ravines. When Marsh arrived, he immediately saw that the general had been right—fossil bones were everywhere. He and his men unearthed more than 2 tons (1.8

Marsh *(left)* and Oglala Sioux leader Red Cloud *(right)* posed for a formal portrait in 1874.

metric tons) of fossils, including many Eocene brontothere bones.

On the expedition's final day, several of Red Cloud's men thundered into camp on horseback. Gesturing fiercely, they told Marsh that warriors from another tribe were coming to attack. Marsh was faced with a hard choice: Should he abandon the fossils and head for safety? Or should he take the time to load the fossils properly onto the wagons—and risk getting caught in an attack? Marsh took the risk. His men packed through the night. At dawn, they headed back to the Red Cloud Agency, where they learned that they'd missed the war party by mere hours.

THE WHEELER SURVEY

Cope had joined the Wheeler survey in 1874. The job paid well and gave him the chance to travel someplace new: New Mexico. However, Cope discovered that army lieutenant George Wheeler was a strict leader, and mapmaking was his survey's priority. When the expedition passed through fossil-rich areas, Wheeler often forbade bone collecting.

Frustrated, Cope tried to get permission by going over Wheeler's head. It didn't work. So one day, as the expedition neared the San Juan River, Cope took off with two guides, a collector, and a packhorse. Near the river's headwaters, he found very old Eocene formations and, as he'd hoped, fossils embedded in the rock. Most were those of ancient mammals, even older than those at Bridger Basin. Cope wrote to his father, "As soon as we picketed horses, we began to find fossil bones! . . . By sundown I had 20 . . . Vertebrates! The most important find in geology I ever made." In five days, Cope collected fossils of seventy-five different types of ancient vertebrate animals.

> "As soon as we picketed horses, we began to find fossil bones! . . . By sundown I had 20 . . . Vertebrates! . . . The most important find in geology I ever made."

E. D. Cope, 1874

When Cope rejoined the survey, Wheeler demanded an explanation. To his surprise, the lieutenant gave Cope more men and mules and told him to keep on collecting. Cope found more primitive mammal fossils and fragments of dinosaur bones. He suspected that the deeper, older rock beneath contained dinosaur fossils. Cope figured that somewhere in the West, rich deposits of dinosaur bones lay close to the surface. He just had to find them.

FREED BY INHERITANCE

Throughout 1875, Cope stayed in Haddonfield working on his San Juan River fossils. It was challenging work, because they came from ancient mammals unlike any previously seen. Cope was frustrated to be stuck at home. But faced with the choice of publishing more than Marsh or doing more fieldwork, Cope chose to keep ahead of his rival by churning out new publications and naming new species.

When Cope's father died, he inherited a fortune and was suddenly free to live and work as he pleased. He moved to Philadelphia and bought two adjacent houses, one for his family and the other for his vast fossil collection. Next, Cope decided to hire professional bone collectors to compete directly with Marsh's men. He hired Charles Hazelius Sternberg. Smart, dedicated, and loyal, Sternberg was a young paleontologist who had briefly studied under Mudge. Cope sent him to western Kansas, near where Mudge and Williston were prospecting for fossils.

Marsh's men and Sternberg worked within a few miles of each other. Their competition for fossils was fierce. Sternberg often spied on Mudge and Williston, noted what they were excavating, and passed the information on to Cope. Mudge and Williston, in turn, kept a close eye on Sternberg and sent regular reports about his activities to Marsh. Working alone, Sternberg was often reluctant to leave a fossil site, even for a few hours, for fear that Mudge and Williston would take it over. Once when Sternberg was running low on food, he discovered a wonderful mosasaur skeleton. But he worried that if he left for supplies, Marsh's men would take it. Sternberg decided to tough

Mosasaurs were large, powerful reptiles that swam in shallow Cretaceous seas. Cope first proposed that snakes and mosasaurs had a common ancestor.

it out, eating nothing but boiled corn for three days so he could hack 800 pounds (363 kilograms) of mosaur bones from the hard, dry ground before his competitors could get them.

By the end of July, Cope was ready to get out into the field himself. Cope suspected the Missouri River basin in north-central Montana might be a good place to look for dinosaur fossils. He set his sights on the Judith River basin.

JUDITH RIVER

Cope, Sternberg, and newly hired fossil hunter J. C. Isaac spent a week reaching the remote outpost of Fort Benton, Montana. There Cope secured a wagon, mules, supplies, a cook, and a guide. Locals cautioned Cope not to go into the Missouri River valley. American Indian warriors were watching for trespassing whites. These warnings worried Isaac, because Indians had killed five of his companions in Wyoming earlier that year. But Cope was confident that he could avoid trouble.

Cope's team followed the Missouri River valley through cliffs, ravines, and rock formations. The rock had once been the floor of the Cretaceous inland sea. Centuries of weathering and river erosion had exposed sediments dating back seventy million years—just before dinosaurs disappeared from Earth.

When the men reached the mouth of the Judith River, they headed east into the Judith River Badlands. There they hunted for bones from sunrise to sunset. Their skin blistered in the heat and swelled with insect bites.

Cope's hunch panned out. They found many bones and teeth of huge fossil reptiles like *Laelaps* and *Hadrosaurus* as well as the nearly complete skeleton of a horned ceratopsid, a dinosaur with a large bony frill extending from its neck. Cope named it *Monoclonius crassus* (thick single-sprout).

THE SECRET
OF COPE'S SUCCESS

Cope's expeditions were usually successful. The key to his success was preparation. Cope read vast numbers of scientific papers, so he knew what fossils others had found and where. For example, he knew that Ferdinand Hayden had sent Joseph Leidy dinosaur bone fragments from the Judith River Badlands in the 1850s. Cope thus believed the area might hold many more dinosaur fossils. Cope visited local amateur fossil hunters, studied their collections, and asked them questions. He also had a gift for imagining ancient landscapes and guessing the best places to look for certain types of fossils.

The dinosaur fossils were extremely fragile, so Cope improvised a method for holding them together. He covered the bones with cloth strips soaked in boiled rice paste. The strips cooled to form a rock-hard casing.

In mid-September, fear of Indian attacks made Cope's cook and guide flee to Fort Benton. But Cope, Sternberg, and Isaac kept searching for fossils for another two weeks. They finally broke camp a few days before the last steamer of the season would depart southward on the Missouri River. With one wagon and a single mule, they transported 1,700 pounds (771 kg) of fossils over miles of rugged terrain, reaching the steamer only just in time.

CHAPTER FIVE

MONSTER
BONES

Cope left Montana certain that somewhere out west lay a treasure trove of dinosaur bones. A few months later, someone found it.

In spring 1877, schoolteacher and amateur geologist Arthur Lakes was exploring with a friend along a creek near Morrison, Colorado, in the Rocky Mountain foothills. The men stumbled across what looked like a fossilized tree trunk. Lakes realized it was a monstrous fossil vertebra nearly 3 feet (1 m) across. He believed it was a dinosaur's but needed an expert opinion.

Lakes wrote to Marsh, who offered to identify the bone, but only if he could see it firsthand. Lakes returned to the site, located more of the gigantic fossils, and dug several out of the ground. He wrote to Marsh again. Not getting an immediate answer, Lakes shipped some of the bones to Yale.

Still Marsh didn't reply. Lakes assumed the Yale paleontologist wasn't interested after all, so he shipped another box of the big bones to Cope. Lakes just wanted someone to identify his fossils—and possibly buy them. But his actions inadvertently triggered the next battle in the Bone Wars.

Days later, Lakes received a letter and a check from Marsh. Lakes quickly dashed off an apology, explaining that he'd also sent bones to Cope. Marsh was furious—and determined that Cope would not share in this new find. He wired Lakes, confirming Yale's strong interest in the fossils, and ordered Mudge to Morrison.

Once there, Mudge hired Lakes and his friend, and ensured that all Morrison bones would go to Marsh after that. Mudge wired Marsh: "Have made satisfactory arrangements for two months. Jones cannot interfere." Jones was a code name for Cope.

But even that wasn't enough for Marsh. He wanted every single bone from Morrison, including those Lakes had already sent to Cope. He insisted that Lakes write to Cope and explain that the bones belonged to Marsh. Unexpectedly, Cope surrendered them without a fight.

THE MORRISON FORMATION

The Morrison formation is the greatest known source of dinosaur fossils in North America. A rock layer found primarily in Colorado and Wyoming, it formed from sediments deposited during the late Jurassic period (161.2 to 145.5 million years ago). Working in the Morrison formation in Colorado and at Como Bluff in Wyoming, Marsh and Cope brought to light some of the most astonishing prehistoric creatures people had ever seen. Many are among the largest animals ever known to have lived on Earth.

Mudge and Lakes organized a major excavation at Morrison. It was difficult work. The rock was hard, and the fossils cracked easily. But the finds were extraordinary. Marsh's first paper about Morrison appeared in the July 1, 1877, issue of the *American Journal of Science*. In it, he described the remains of a Jurassic period sauropod (a huge, long-necked, plant-eating dinosaur): "The entire animal . . . was apparently an herbivorous [plant-eating] reptile, and as it is quite distinct from any hitherto described, the species may be called *Titanosaurus montanus*" (huge mountain lizard). Marsh's *Titanosaurus* replaced Cope's *Agathaumas* as the largest dinosaur known.

> "These dimensions would indicate for the entire animal a length of probably 50 to 60 feet [15 to 18 m]. It was apparently an herbivorous [plant–eating] reptile, and as it is quite distinct from any hitherto described, the species may be called *Titanosaurus montanus*."
>
> O. C. Marsh, 1877

In an 1877 article, Marsh identified a huge sauropod as one of the fossil finds from the Morrison formation in Wyoming. This 1934 photo of the formation shows sauropod fossils in the same area.

NAMING
ERRORS

In his first paper about Morrison, Marsh mentioned finding bones of another *Laelaps*, the species Cope discovered at Haddonfield in 1866. Marsh noted an error Cope had made in naming the animal: "This name *Laelaps* is preoccupied [already taken], having been used . . . in 1835, and again . . . in 1843. It may, therefore, be replaced by *Dryptosaurus*." With this comment, Marsh displayed amazing arrogance: he took the liberty of renaming Cope's first dinosaur discovery. Shortly thereafter, Cope pointed out that the name of Marsh's *Titanosaurus* was already taken too. At least Cope left renaming *Titanosaurus* to Marsh, who chose *Atlantosaurus*, which has a similar meaning.

COPE'S COUP

Cope didn't mind surrendering the Morrison bones because he was getting bigger and better ones elsewhere. Another Colorado schoolteacher, O. W. Lucas, had found more monster bones near Cañon City, about 100 miles (161 kilometers) south of Morrison. Lucas had written Cope about his discovery. When samples arrived, Cope was elated. The fossils were definitely Jurassic sauropods. Cope hired Lucas and a team to dig at Cañon City. Cope's first major discovery from Cañon City, a sauropod he called *Camarasaurus* (chambered lizard), was bigger than Marsh's *Titanosaurus*. To irritate Marsh, Cope wrote that *Camarasaurus* "exceeds in its proportions any other land animal hitherto discovered, including the one found . . . by Professor Lakes."

Outraged, Marsh ordered Mudge to hurry down to Cañon City and investigate. Mudge reported Cope's fossils were not only bigger than Marsh's but also in better condition and buried in softer rock. Marsh's team often used dynamite to get at the fossils. Cope's team only had to use picks and

This 1879 photo shows excavated dinosaur bones found near Cañon City, Colorado, where Cope found huge dinosaur bones in the late 1870s. Excavation techniques were fairly crude at the time, and these bones are in amazingly good shape.

shovels to extract largely intact specimens from the rock.

The competition intensified. Each team worked feverishly to unearth fossils as quickly as possible. In early August, Marsh's men discovered a 75-foot (23 m) sauropod he named *Apatosaurus* (deceptive lizard). It was the longest land animal ever found.

Cope's men at Cañon City soon came across bones of a sauropod he dubbed *Amphicoelias* (double hollow). It was the world's tallest known dinosaur. Marsh's team countered with one of the strangest-looking dinosaurs ever seen: a 30-foot (10 m) spiky-tailed creature with triangular bony plates jutting up from its arched back. Marsh named it *Stegosaurus* (roof lizard).

With such stupendous discoveries at stake, each camp was shrouded in secrecy. The two teams of fossil hunters spied on each other constantly and communicated with their respective employers using coded messages.

> "[*Camarasaurus*] exceeds in its proportions any other land animal hitherto discovered, including the one found... by Professor Lakes."
>
> E. D. Cope, 1877

A MYSTERIOUS LETTER

Thanks to the discoveries at Morrison, Marsh had dinosaur fever. When he received a mysterious letter in early August from two Wyoming men about the discovery of huge fossil bones—bigger than any in Colorado—he was intrigued. The men, who gave their names as Harlow and Edwards, wanted to sell the bones. Although Marsh was skeptical, he wired back, requesting fossils for examination.

When the fossils arrived at Yale, Marsh was ecstatic to find that they were indeed dinosaur bones. He sent Williston to Wyoming right away. Williston learned that Harlow and Edwards were actually William Harlow Reed and William Edwards Carlin. They worked at the tiny rail stop of Como, Wyoming.

Reed and Carlin took Williston to nearby Como Bluff, a long, low ridge in a bleak landscape. Williston saw why the men had been so guarded. Fossils littered the ground as far as the eye could see. Williston dashed off an excited letter to Marsh: "Cañon City and Morrison are simply nowhere in comparison with this locality both as regards perfection, accessibility, and quantity." But, he added, "There will be great danger next summer of competition."

COMO BLUFF

Marsh wanted desperately to keep Como Bluff for himself. But he soon learned that someone had informed the Smithsonian about the bones there, and the institution had, in turn, notified Cope. Marsh had to work fast. He hired Carlin and Reed, who agreed to dig fossils secretly and try to keep other bone hunters away from Como Bluff. Williston put Reed in charge and left.

When winter came, Reed and Carlin battled subzero temperatures and savage winds as they dug and hauled bones from the bluff to the station, packed up crates, and loaded them into train cars. Reed was a hard worker. Carlin was not. As the weeks passed, Carlin grew lazier, and Reed grew tired of doing most of the work.

Back at Yale, Marsh opened box after box of amazing specimens from Como Bluff. Many were new species, such as *Diplodocus* (double beam), a sauropod with a long, whiplike tail, and *Allosaurus* (different lizard), a large predator with powerful hind legs, a colossal head, and dozens of sharp teeth. Marsh wrote up his findings as fast as he could.

However, in April 1878, an article about Marsh and the rich fossil fields at Como Bluff appeared in Wyoming's *Laramie Daily Sentinel*. Marsh suspected Carlin had leaked the information, so he sent Williston to silence the man—and to be there if Cope showed up. When a stranger named Haines appeared at Como, asking questions, Williston suspected him of being a spy for Cope. He wrote to Marsh, "There is no doubt that he [Haines] is direct from Cope . . . didn't mention Cope's name, but [mentioned] yours frequently, rather disparagingly [negatively]."

Como Bluff in Wyoming yielded exciting new dinosaur finds, including *Allosaurus* bones like these.

Day after day, the team dug fossils. Some of the bones were as thick as trees and longer than the men were tall. By summer's end, Marsh had nearly 30 tons (27 metric tons) of fossils from Como Bluff. And Cope still had not shown up.

"There is no doubt that he [Haines] is direct from Cope... didn't mention Cope's name, but yours [Marsh's] frequently, rather disparagingly [negatively]."

Sam Williston, referring to a man he suspected of spying on Marsh's team at Como Bluff, 1878

DISASTER LOOMS

In summer 1878, changes that could affect paleontology for years to come were afoot in Washington, D.C., so Marsh stayed in the city to make sure the changes worked in his favor. Congress was unhappy with the four U.S. geological surveys of the West because they tended to map the same areas and give different names to the same features. The overlap wasted money and caused confusion. For help in streamlining the surveys, Congress turned to the National Academy of Sciences (NAS). Marsh had become president of NAS in May 1878.

Marsh appointed a committee to investigate, and he strongly influenced its final recommendation to Congress. The committee advised creating a single government survey with one director and several key scientific positions, including a chief paleontologist. The committee suggested Marsh for the job.

Cope was devastated by the news. The surveys had paid for his fossil collecting and published many of his discoveries in their reports. In addition, Cope was just completing an enormous book on paleontology. He was counting on its publication at government expense, since he'd done much of the research under the Hayden survey. But if Marsh became chief paleontologist of a single government survey, Cope knew he would be cut out of the field entirely.

Cope asked sympathetic NAS colleagues to counter the committee's recommendations but to no avail. On March 21, 1879, Congress decided there would be one survey, the United States Geological Survey (USGS), led by Clarence King.

Cope knew King was sure to name Marsh chief paleontologist. That meant he'd never work on a government-funded survey again. But Cope didn't lie down in defeat. Instead, he took the fight to Como Bluff.

TREACHERY AND TREASURES

In spring 1879, Marsh got alarming news from Wyoming. Carlin had started digging at a new site and was shipping fossils—to Cope! Carlin had gone so far as to bar Reed from using the station to crate Marsh's fossils.

With Reed working for Marsh and Carlin for Cope, Reed and Carlin constantly tried to bully each other. Neither man would let the other come near where he was working. They pitched tents over their digs to hide any fossils from view. The competition became so vicious that Marsh was willing to sacrifice scientific progress for his own personal pride. When Reed was finished digging at a site, Marsh ordered him to smash any remaining fossils—precious records of Earth's history—so Carlin, and ultimately Cope, couldn't get them.

Marsh came out to Como Bluff for a few days in early June. He visited several digging sites, astounded by the fossil treasures they contained. He urged his men to work harder and get as many fossils as possible for him and the Peabody Museum.

Cope visited in early August. He wrote to Julia that "the boys have dug out a huge flesh-eating saurian which they send off this morning." It turned out to be one of the most complete *Allosaurus* skeletons ever found.

Como Bluff also yielded a vast array of fossils of small reptiles, amphibians, and mammals. Few of these little mammals were larger than a rat. But the collectors were impressed with the variety of species. These fossils were proof that a great assortment of small

> "The boys have dug out a huge flesh–eating saurian which they send off this morning."
>
> E. D. Cope, at Como Bluff, 1879

mammals had lived alongside dinosaurs during the Jurassic period. Marsh and Cope also realized that some of these small creatures were likely the ancestors of the much larger Eocene mammals whose bones they'd found at Bridger Basin and elsewhere. All this was more dramatic proof as to how life had changed and diversified throughout Earth's long history.

MARSH'S BIG MISTAKE

In their quest to claim the best, the biggest, the most, and the most unusual fossils at Como Bluff, Cope and Marsh made many mistakes. They rushed their analyses. They misidentified some fossils and hurriedly named others. They wrote papers that introduced those mistakes into the scientific literature—mistakes that other paleontologists took years to correct.

For example, Reed sent Marsh a fairly complete skeleton of a giant sauropod 70 to 80 feet (21 to 24 m) long from Como Bluff. Marsh hastily dubbed it a new species, *Brontosaurus* (thunder lizard). He wanted to display it at the Peabody Museum. Marsh completed the skeleton with bones he assumed were from other brontosaurs found at Como Bluff, including a massive skull. Marsh's mounted *Brontosaurus* became a world-famous dinosaur.

In fact, *Brontosaurus* was actually a very large *Apatosaurus*—with a skull from a *Camarasaurus*! This mistake wasn't discovered until 1903—years after Marsh and Cope had died. But *Brontosaurus* was so beloved by the public that it lived on in books and in museum displays until the late 1900s.

CHAPTER SIX

FINAL CONFRONTATION

By summer 1881, Como Bluff was crawling with fossil hunters. To compete, Marsh expanded his team. As expected, the USGS—now led by John Wesley Powell— had named Marsh its chief paleontologist.

Marsh received a handsome salary, plus additional money for research, fossil collecting, and a large staff. He was poised to become the United States' premier paleontologist—and a wealthy man.

Cope, on the other hand, was struggling. He'd spent nearly all his inheritance on expeditions, fossil-hunting teams, and several costly fossil collections. As Cope's fortune dwindled, so did his access to new fossils. And with no new fossils to study and publish papers about, he couldn't compete with Marsh professionally.

By the mid-1880s, Cope was in dire financial straits. He applied for jobs at the Smithsonian and the American Museum of Natural History. Both turned

In this 1897 illustration, based on a photograph, Cope sits in his office surrounded by pieces of his vast fossil collection. A ploy by Marsh to force Cope to surrender his collection triggered the last chapter in the Bone Wars.

him down. He sought university professorships. Because of Cope's combative reputation, however, no one wanted to hire him.

Yet Cope kept writing. He'd finished his massive book on paleontology in 1883. *The Vertebrata of the Tertiary Formations of the West*—or "Cope's Bible," as it came to be called—was a masterpiece. It contained more than one thousand pages of text and seventy-five detailed illustrations. Government funds left over from the Hayden survey had financed its publication.

Cope had begun a second volume. Together, the two books would represent his life's work. Yet he couldn't afford to publish the second book on his own. When he asked the USGS for funds to do so, Powell refused. Cope suspected that Marsh had influenced Powell's decision. Blocking publication of Cope's second book gave Marsh a chance to publish his own findings about certain fossils first.

In 1885 Cope asked Congress for help. Several congressional representatives introduced a bill that would have provided funds for publication. The bill didn't pass, however. Cope tried again. The bill failed a second time and then a third. Cope believed that Powell and Marsh were to blame and decided to retaliate.

COPE ATTACKS

Powell had political enemies in Washington who were looking to discredit him. Cope hoped to win friends by providing these men with evidence of USGS mismanagement. Cope and several other former members of the Hayden survey wrote a detailed report attacking Powell and the USGS and circulated it through Congress. In a congressional hearing called to investigate the report's allegations, Powell defended himself well. In fact, he so brilliantly countered Cope's accusations that he won even more support from Congress.

When Cope's first attack failed, he turned his angry attention to Marsh and his staff. Marsh had many people working for him: fossil collectors, technicians who prepared bones for study, illustrators, and researchers. Marsh relied heavily on all his employees, but especially his researchers. He listened to their analyses and used that information in his scientific papers. Marsh rarely credited them for their efforts. He even forbade them from publishing articles of their own. And he paid embarrassingly small salaries. As a result, several of Marsh's employees—past and present—loathed him.

Cope sought out these people. He met with them secretly and recorded many pages of testimony on Marsh's scientific failings and unethical behavior. Cope called this information his "Marshiana." When he showed the documents to friend and fellow paleontologist Henry Fairfield Osborn, Cope said, "Here is my accumulated store of Marshiana. In these papers I have a full record of Marsh's errors from the very beginning, which at some future time I may be tempted to publish."

Meanwhile, Cope's financial situation worsened. In 1888 he took out loans and borrowed money from friends. He tried to sell some of his most valuable fossils. But he didn't give up his attack on Marsh.

In April 1889, Marsh ran for reelection as NAS president. Cope mounted a nasty campaign against him, using some of his Marshiana to try to ruin Marsh's scientific standing. His effort backfired. Cope's viciousness appalled even those who disliked Marsh, and Marsh easily won reelection.

FIGHT IN THE PRESS

In fall 1889, the University of Pennsylvania offered Cope a job as a geology professor. Things seemed to be looking up until December, when Cope received a letter from the U.S. Secretary of the Interior. The letter ordered Cope to surrender his fossil collection to the Smithsonian, claiming it was government property acquired under the Hayden survey.

The demand was outrageous, likely initiated by Marsh through Powell. Without his fossils, Cope would be ruined. His seething hatred for Marsh led him to take his story to the press.

Cope turned over all his Marshiana to a writer for the *New York Herald*. The *Herald*'s publisher saw a big opportunity. Because the public had fossil fever too, he hoped Cope's story would sell a lot of newspapers. In an era before radio, television, and the Internet, newspapers were key sources of information.

The first article appeared on January 12, 1890, under the headline "Scientists Wage Bitter Warfare." The article claimed that Marsh did little of his own research, that errors riddled his publications, and that he took credit for others' work. It also asserted that Marsh had used political friendships to secure his USGS position and that he was unfit to be NAS president.

The article also lambasted Powell and USGS, calling it a "gigantic politico-scientific monopoly." The story ended with an explanation from Cope: he was publicizing these issues because the government had demanded he surrender his fossil collection.

Cope was pleased with the article. "You have seen Sunday's *Herald*," he wrote to Osborn. "Either he [Marsh] or I must go under. . . . I have, I believe, performed an unpleasant but necessary duty to my country."

To avoid being sued, the *Herald* had sent advance copies of the article to Marsh and Powell, inviting them to respond. In Powell's reply, he countered Cope's accusations. He said, "In addition to his [Cope's] great vanity . . . he is inordinately [unusually] jealous and suspicious. . . . In fact, his general ravings about scientific men . . . whom he believes are all in league against himself, make it impossible for him to associate on terms of cooperation."

Marsh's reply came one week later, and it took up an entire page. Marsh rebutted all Cope's accusations. He went on to list Cope's mistakes one by one, from Cope's snooping at Como Bluff to his 1869 *Elasmosaurus* blunder. Marsh made it clear that he believed Cope was an incompetent liar. He closed with, "Has Professor Cope since learned wisdom from his increasing years? The public must judge. The scientific world has long since passed judgment."

"Either he [Marsh] or I must go under. . . . I have, I believe, performed an unpleasant but necessary duty to my country."

E. D. Cope, referring to his accusations about Marsh in the *New York Herald*, 1890

"Has Professor Cope since learned wisdom from his increasing years? The public must judge. The scientific world has long since passed judgment."

O. C. Marsh, responding to Cope's attack in the *New York Herald*, January 19, 1890

BEYOND THE BATTLE

The debate eventually fizzled, but not without earning Cope some sympathy. Government officials retracted the demand for his fossil collection. In 1892 Congress severely slashed USGS funding. Powell soon resigned, and Marsh's position was eliminated. He had to ask Yale to pay him a salary.

While Cope had finally gotten his revenge, it came at a huge cost to science. Paleontology lost much of its government funding, which meant that fossil studies slowed dramatically.

In the last years of his life, Cope continued writing at a remarkable pace. He died April 12, 1897, at the age of fifty-six. Marsh finished his career at Yale. He died March 19, 1899, at the age of sixty-seven. Marsh and Cope never reconciled. They remained mutual enemies until death.

LEGACY

The Bone Wars left quite a legacy. Marsh and Cope became legends—for both their bitter rivalry and for their remarkable scientific contributions. On the one hand, the Bone Wars were damaging. They established a climate of mistrust and deception among scientists and tarnished the United States' scientific reputation for decades. The vicious bickering drove Joseph Leidy out of paleontology. The rivalry also crippled the USGS, slowing the pace of paleontological research. In their haste to outdo each other, Marsh and Cope both did some shoddy work. They often described new species based on sparse evidence, sometimes incorrectly. Occasionally they mixed up bones from different animals. The resulting confusion took many years to sort out.

This 1880 letter from Charles Darwin to Marsh praises Marsh's fossil discoveries as excellent evidence to support the theory of evolution by natural selection.

animals of N. America has afforded the best support to the theory of evolution, which has appeared within the last 20 years. The general appearance of the copy which you have sent me is worthy of its contents, and I can say nothing stronger than this.

On the other hand, the Bone Wars benefited paleontology. When Cope and Marsh began their careers, scientists knew little about dinosaurs. Together, the two men discovered and described more than 130 dinosaur species. Both also discovered many ancient mammals and other vertebrates. Their work generated keen public interest in prehistoric life and provided a firm foundation for the generations of paleontologists who followed.

Marsh, in particular, found fossil evidence that supported Darwin's theory of evolution. Marsh's finds helped fill gaps in the fossil record, showing how features in living things changed over time. His collection of ancient horse fossils became a key example of evolutionary progression. His discovery and analysis of ancient toothed birds strongly suggested that modern birds descended from small dinosaurs.

Cope's paleontological interests were wider ranging than Marsh's. Among his many contributions were his New Mexico fossil discoveries,

Through their life's work, Marsh and Cope expanded scientific knowledge about dinosaurs enormously. Shown here is Marsh's 1896 illustration of a *Stegosaurus*.

which demonstrated that mammals appeared earlier than scholars had previously thought. Few scientists in any field have rivaled Cope's volume of writing. He published nearly fourteen hundred scientific papers and several groundbreaking books. These included not only *Vertebrata* but also books about the natural history of reptiles and amphibians. In 1913 the scientific society for research on fish, amphibians, and reptiles named its journal *Copeia* in Cope's honor.

History will always remember Othniel Charles Marsh and Edward Drinker Cope for their great rivalry. This rivalry brought out the best and the worst in them—while bringing humankind a brand-new view of ancient life on Earth.

TIMELINE

1831	Othniel Charles Marsh is born in Lockport, New York.
1840	Edward Drinker Cope is born outside Philadelphia, Pennsylvania.
1858	Joseph Leidy reports on the finding of *Hadrosaurus foulkii*.
1859	Charles Darwin publishes *On the Origin of Species by Means of Natural Selection*.
1860	Cope attends Leidy's lectures at the University of Pennsylvania. Marsh collects fossil vertebrae of *Eosaurus acadianus* in Nova Scotia.
1863	Cope and Marsh meet in Berlin.
1866	Cope discovers *Laelaps aquilunguis*. The Peabody Museum is founded at Yale.
1868	Cope moves to Haddonfield. Marsh makes his first visit to the West and collects fossils at Antelope Junction.
1869	Cope reconstructs *Elasmosaurus*. Marsh points out Cope's mistaken positioning of *Elasmosaurus*'s head.
1870	Marsh leads the first Yale expedition.
1871	Marsh leads the second Yale expedition. Cope makes his first fossil-hunting trip to the West.
1872	Cope and Marsh compete for fossils at Bridger Basin in Wyoming.
1873	Cope and Marsh conduct their "war of words" in the *American Naturalist*.
1874	Cope finds fossils with the Wheeler survey. Construction begins on the Peabody Museum. Marsh collects fossils in the White River Badlands.
1876	Cope explores the Judith River Badlands.
1877	Dinosaur fossils are discovered at Morrison and Cañon City, Colorado.
1878	William Harlow Reed and William Edwards Carlin sign an agreement with Marsh to collect fossils at Como Bluff.
1879	The four government surveys are consolidated into one U.S. Geological Survey. Cope and Marsh both have fossil-collecting teams working at Como Bluff.
1885	Cope mounts a campaign to discredit John Wesley Powell and the USGS.
1886 - 1888	A congressional bill for funding to publish Cope's second volume fails.
1890	Cope and Marsh publish accusations and rebuttals in the *New York Herald*.
1892	Marsh is forced to resign as chief paleontologist with the USGS.
1897	Cope dies.
1899	Marsh dies.

Handwritten annotations:
- (next to 1863): married annie 8/15/65
- (next to 1866): outing w/ Marsh in March
- (next to 1868): Aug. 1 / Haddonfield
- (next to 1869): Cardiff Oct/Nov
- (next to 1872): + Leidy

GLOSSARY

ceratopsid: a group of plant-eating Cretaceous dinosaurs that had beaklike jaws and elaborate horns and bony neck frills. *Triceratops* is a well-known ceratopsid.

classify: to group in categories based on similarities. Scientists classify living things using eight ranks of categories. From smallest to largest, the ranks are species, genus, family, order, class, phylum, kingdom, and domain. Similar species make up a genus, similar genera make up a family, and so on.

evolution: gradual change over time. Charles Darwin's theory of evolution—as described in his 1859 book, *On the Origin of Species by Means of Natural Selection*—proposes that living things evolve through a process called natural selection. Members of the same species are born with random genetic variations that cause variety in physical traits. Individuals with traits better suited to their environment are more likely to survive, reproduce, and pass on their traits.

fossil: preserved remains or traces of animals, plants, and other organisms from Earth's distant past

marine sediment: particles of rock, soil, or tiny ocean organisms that accumulate on the seafloor

mosasaur: a large reptile that flourished in the oceans of the late Cretaceous period. Mosasaurs were meat-eating predators that breathed air and gave birth to live young. They ranged from about 10 feet (3 m) to 57 feet (17 m) long.

naturalist: a person who studies plants and animals primarily by observing and comparing them, rather than by doing experiments

paleontology: the study, especially through fossils, of prehistoric life and how organisms evolve

plesiosaur: an aquatic reptile that lived during the Jurassic and Cretaceous periods. Plesiosaurs had short tails, broad bodies, and flippers. Some, such as *Elasmosaurus*, had long necks. They were meat-eating predators that gave birth to live young.

sauropod: a very large type of plant-eating land dinosaur that lived during the Jurassic and Cretaceous periods. Sauropods had small heads, long necks and tails, and trunklike legs. Sauropods were Earth's largest known land animals, ranging from about 20 feet (6 m) to 190 feet (58 m) long.

SOURCE NOTES

7   George Bird Grinnell, "Othniel Charles Marsh," *Leading Men in American Science*, ed. David Starr Jordan (New York: Henry Holt & Company, 1910), 286.

7   Ibid.

11 Henry Fairfield Osborn, *Cope: Master Naturalist* (New York: Arno Press, 1978), 108.

11 Ibid.

15 Peabody Museum of Natural History, "The O. C. Marsh Story," *Yale Peabody Museum of Natural History*, 2011, http://peabody .yale.edu/collections/archives/oc-marsh-story (August 3, 2011).

18 Charles Schuchert and Clara Mae LeVene, *O. C. Marsh: Pioneer in Paleontology* (New York: Arno Press, 1978), 120.

19 Ibid.

21 Osborn, *Cope*, 162.

21 Ibid.

28 O. C. Marsh, "Fossil Mammals of the Order Dinocerata," *American Naturalist* 7, no. 3 (March 1873); 152, available online at http://www.jstor.org/stable/2448343?seq= 7&Search=yes&searchText=unfortunate&se archText=likewise&searchText=especially& searchText=attributing&searchText=Dinoce rata&list=hide&searchUri=%2Faction%2Fd oBasicSearch%3Ffilter%3D%26Query%3D He%2Bhas%2Blikewise%2Bbeen%2Bespe cially%2Bunfortunate%2Bin%2Battributing %2Bto%2Bthe%2BDinocerata%2B%26wc %3Don%26Search.x%3D0%26Search.y%3 D0&prevSearch=&item=1&ttl=2&returnArt icleService=showFullText&resultsServiceNa me=null (April 17, 2012).

28 Ibid.

29 E. D. Cope, "On Some of Professor Marsh's Criticisms," *American Naturalist* 7, no. 5 (May 1873); 298, , available online at http://www.jstor.org/stable/2448303?seq= 9&Search=yes&searchText=Marsh%27s&s earchText=Prof.&searchText=criticisms&sea rchText=plain&searchText=misrepresentatio ns&list=hide&searchUri=%2Faction%2Fdo BasicSearch%3Ffilter%3D%26Query%3Dit %2Bis%2Bplain%2Bthat%2Bmost%2Bof% 2BProf.%2BMarsh%25E2%2580%2599s% 2Bcriticisms%2Bare%2Bmisrepresentations %26wc%3Don%26Search.x%3D0%26Sea rch.y%3D0&prevSearch=&item=1&ttl=1&r eturnArticleService=showFullText&resultsS erviceName=null (April 17, 2012).

29 Ibid.

33 Osborn, *Cope*, 201.

33 Ibid.

39 Mark Jaffe, *The Gilded Dinosaur: The Fossil War Between E. D. Cope and O. C. Marsh and the Rise of American Science* (New York: Crown Publishers, 2000), 189.

40 O. C. Marsh, "Notice of a New and Gigantic Dinosaur," *American Journal of Science*, 14, no. 3 (1877): 88.

40 Ibid.

41 Ibid.

41 Osborn, *Cope*, 256.

42 Ibid.

43 Jaffe, *Gilded Dinosaur*, 229.

44 David Rains Wallace, *The Bonehunters' Revenge: Dinosaurs, Greed, and the Greatest Scientific Feud of the Gilded Age* (Boston: Houghton Mifflin, 1999), 152.

45 Ibid.

46 Jaffe, *Gilded Dinosaur*, 243 (Cope correspondence, letter 203, August 8, 1879).

46 Ibid.

50 Osborn, *Cope*, 585.

51 Wallace, *Bonehunters' Revenge*, 217.

51 Marcia L. Thomas, "John Wesley Powell: White Water to White City," *Illinois Wesleyan University Digital Commons*, 2007, http://digitalcommons.iwu.edu/cgi/

viewcontent.cgi?article=1004&context =ames_scholarship (September 2, 2011).

51 Osborn, *Cope*, 410.

52 Ibid.

52 Wallace, *Bonehunters' Revenge*, 224.

52 Ibid., 245.

52 Ibid.

SELECTED BIBLIOGRAPHY

Academy of Natural Sciences. "Joseph Leidy Online Exhibit." *Academy of Natural Sciences*. N.d. http://www.ansp.org/museum/leidy/index.php (September 8, 2011).

Clowes, Chris, Mikko Haaramo, M. Alan Kazlev, Roger Perkins, Renato Felipe Vidal Santos, Christopher Taylor, and Toby White. *Palaeos: Life Through Deep Time*. N.d. http://palaeos.com (March 12, 2012).

Colbert, Edwin H. *The Great Dinosaur Hunters and Their Discoveries*. New York: Dover Publications, 1984.

Conklin, Edwin G. "The Early History of the American Naturalist." *JSTOR*. December 29, 1942. http://www.jstor.org/userimages/ContentEditor/1290226970053/early-history.pdf (September 8, 2011).

Cope, E. D. "On Some of Professor Marsh's Criticisms." *American Naturalist* 7, no. 5 (May 1873): 290–299.

Davidson, Jane Pierce. *The Bone Sharp: The Life of Edward Drinker Cope*. Philadelphia: Academy of Natural Sciences, 1997.

Frazer, Persifor. "The Life and Letters of Edward Drinker Cope." *American Geologist* 26, no. 2 (August 1900): 67–128.

Jaffe, Mark. *The Gilded Dinosaur: The Fossil War Between E. D. Cope and O. C. Marsh and the Rise of American Science*. New York: Crown Publishers, 2000.

Kohl, Michael F., and John S. McIntosh, eds. *Discovering Dinosaurs in the Old West: The Field Journals of Arthur Lakes*. Washington, DC: Smithsonian Institution Press, 1997.

Lanham, Url. *The Bone Hunters*. New York: Columbia University Press, 1973.

Marsh, O. C. "Description of the Remains of a New Enaliosaurian (*Eosaurus Acadianus*), from the Coal-Formation of Nova Scotia." *Quarterly Journal of the Geological Society* 19, no. 1–2 (1863): 52–56.

————. "Fossil Mammals of the Order Dinocerata," *American Naturalist* 7, no. 3 (March 1873): 146–153.

Osborn, Henry Fairfield. "Biographical Memoir of Edward Drinker Cope 1840–1897." *National Academy of Sciences Biographical Memoirs* 13, no. 3 (1929): 127–317.

————. *Cope: Master Naturalist*. New York: Arno Press, 1978.

Ostrom, John H., and John S. McIntosh. *Marsh's Dinosaurs: The Collections from Como Bluff*. New Haven, CT: Yale University Press, 1966.

Penick, James. "Professor Cope vs. Professor Marsh." *American Heritage*, August 1971. http://www.americanheritage.com/content/professor-cope-vs-professor-marsh (September 8, 2011).

Perkins, Roger. *The Virtual Fossil Museum*. N.d. http://www.fossilmuseum.net (September 8, 2011).

Plate, Robert. *The Dinosaur Hunters: Othniel C. Marsh and Edward D. Cope*. New York: McKay, 1964.

Regents of the University of California, *The Dinosauria*. N.d. http://www.ucmp.berkeley.edu/diapsids /dinosaur.html (September 8, 2011).

Schuchert, Charles. "Biographical Memoir of Othniel Charles Marsh 1831–1899." *National Academy of Sciences Biographical Memoirs* 20, no. 1 (1938): 1–80.

Schuchert, Charles, and Clara Mae LeVene. *O. C. Marsh: Pioneer in Paleontology*. New York: Arno Press, 1978.

Trimble, Donald E. "The Geologic Story of the Great Plains." *North Dakota State University Library*. 1980. http://library.ndsu.edu/exhibits/text/greatplains/text.html (September 8, 2011).

Wallace, David Rains. *The Bonehunters' Revenge: Dinosaurs, Greed, and the Greatest Scientific Feud of the Gilded Age*. Boston: Houghton Mifflin, 1999.

FURTHER READING AND WEBSITES

BOOKS

Brinkman, Paul D. *The Second Jurassic Dinosaur Rush: Museums and Paleontology in America at the Turn of the Twentieth Century*. Chicago: University of Chicago Press, 2010.

Dingus, Lowell, Luis M. Chiappe, and Rodolfo Coria. *Dinosaur Eggs Discovered! Unscrambling the Clues*. Minneapolis: Twenty-First Century Books, 2008.

Emling, Shelley. *The Fossil Hunter: Dinosaurs, Evolution, and the Woman Whose Discoveries Changed the World*. Basingstoke, UK: Palgrave Macmillan, 2011.

Fleisher, Paul. *Evolution*. Minneapolis: Twenty-First Century Books, 2006.

Hellman, Hal. *Great Feuds in Science: Ten of the Liveliest Disputes Ever*. New York: John Wiley and Sons, 1998.

Holtz, Thomas R. *Dinosaurs: The Most Complete, Up-to-Date Encyclopedia for Dinosaur Lovers of All Ages*. New York: Random House, 2007.

Krull, Kathleen. *Charles Darwin*. New York: Viking, 2010.

Naish, Darren. *The Great Dinosaur Discoveries*. Berkeley: University of California Press, 2009.

Ottaviani, Jim. *Bone Sharps, Cowboys, and Thunder Lizards: A Tale of Edward Drinker Cope, Othniel Charles Marsh, and the Gilded Age of Paleontology*. Ann Arbor, MI: G. T. Labs, 2005.

Paul, Gregory S. *The Princeton Field Guide to Dinosaurs*. Princeton, NJ: Princeton University Press, 2010.

Ray, Deborah, Kogan. *Dinosaur Mountain: Digging into the Jurassic Age*. New York: Farrar, Straus and Giroux, 2010.

Silverstein, Alvin, Virginia Silverstein, and Laura Silverstein Nunn. *Adaptation*. Minneapolis: Twenty-First Century Books, 2008.

Stewart, Melissa. *Classification of Life*. Minneapolis: Twenty-First Century Books, 2008.

Wood, A. J. *Charles Darwin and the Beagle Adventure*. Dorking, UK: Templar, 2009.

WEBSITES

"Bone Wars: The Cope-Marsh Rivalry"
http://www.ansp.org/museum/leidy/paleo/bone_wars.php
Read a synopsis of the famous scientific rivalry and then check out dozens of other links on this website to learn more about paleontology, paleontologists, and key fossil finds in North America.

"The Dinosauria"
http://www.ucmp.berkeley.edu/diapsids/dinosaur.html
Explore this site to learn about dinosaur finds and the fossil record, major groups of dinosaurs, dinosaur habitats and diets, and more.

Dinosaur Wars
http://www.pbs.org/wgbh/americanexperience/films/dinosaur/player/
Watch a historical documentary produced for public television about the famous rivalry between Cope and Marsh.

DinoViewer
http://dsc.discovery.com/dinosaurs/dinosaur-games/dinosaur-viewer/dinosaur-viewer.html
With the click of a mouse, you can view several dozen dinosaurs from different continents in great detail, including 360 degree views and size comparisons.

Paper Dinosaurs
http://www.lindahall.org/events_exhib/exhibit/exhibits/dino/index.shtml
Explore printed materials including original papers—with illustrations—written by Cope, Marsh, Leidy, and other famous bone hunters of the nineteenth and early twentieth centuries.

Smithsonian National Museum of Natural History: Dinosaurs
http://paleobiology.si.edu/dinosaurs/index.htm
The Smithsonian has housed many important North American fossils since the mid-1800s. When O. C. Marsh died, all the fossils he'd collected for the government during his lifetime went to the Smithsonian's Department of Vertebrate Fossils. This website provides a wealth of information about dinosaurs and the Smithsonian's collections and offers virtual tours of museum exhibits and a dinosaur dig.

LERNER

SOURCE

Expand learning beyond the printed book. Download free, complementary educational resources for this book from our website, www.lerneresource.com.

INDEX

PHOTO ACKNOWLEDGMENTS

The images in this book are used with the permission of: © Science Faction/SuperStock, pp. 5 (left), 21, 32; © Science, Industry and Business Library/New York Public Library/Photo Researchers, Inc., p. 5 (right); © Science & Society Picture Library/Getty Images, p. 6; © Thomas Kitchin & Victoria Hurst/First Light/Getty Images, p. 8; © Universal Images Group/SuperStock, p. 9; Library of Congress, p. 11 (LC-D4-71086); © Laura Westlund/Independent Picture Service, pp. 13, 27; Courtesy of the Peabody Museum of Natural History, Yale University, New Haven, Connecticut, USA., pp. 17, 53; © age fotostock/SuperStock, p. 18; U.S. Geological Survey/photo by William Henry Jackson, pp. 22–23; © Nature Source/Photo Researchers, Inc., pp. 25, 54; © Kevin Schafer/CORBIS, p. 31; © Richard T. Nowitz/Photo Researchers, Inc., p. 35; U.S. Geological Survey/photo by G. E. Lewis, p. 40; © Royal Gorge Regional Museum & History Center, p. 42; © Ambient Images Inc./SuperStock, p. 44; © North Wind Picture Archives, p. 49.

Front cover: © Phil Degginger/Alamy.

Main body text set in Frutiger LT Std 11/15. Typeface provided by Adobe Systems.

ABOUT THE AUTHOR

Rebecca L. Johnson is an author with a passion for science. She's written more than seventy-five books for kids and young adults, and a few for adults too. Her books have received awards from *Scientific American*, the National Science Teachers Association, the Children's Book Council, the Society of School Librarians International, the New York Public Library, and others.